Demeter and Persephone, the Seasons of Time

Written by I. M. Richardson
Illustrated by Robert Baxter

Troll Associates

Library of Congress Cataloging in Publication Data

Richardson, I. M.
  Demeter and Persephone, the seasons of time.

  Summary: Hades, the god of the dead, falls in
love with Persephone, the maiden of spring, and
steals her from her mother Demeter to be his
bride and queen of the underworld.
  1. Demeter (Greek deity)—Juvenile literature.
2. Persephone (Greek deity)—Juvenile literature.
[1. Mythology, Greek. 2. Demeter (Greek deity)
3. Persephone (Greek deity)] I. Baxter, Robert,
1930-   ill. II. Title.
BL820.C5R5 1983   292'.211   82-16023
ISBN 0-89375-863-9
ISBN 0-89375-864-7 (pbk.)

10   9   8   7   6   5   4   3   2

Hades, the god of the dead, looked closely at Mount Aetna. Beneath it was buried a fire-breathing monster, who was threatening to split the mountain wide open. Even the smallest crack would allow the sun to shine down into the dismal gloom of the underworld. But Hades saw no signs that this would happen yet.

Hades did not often venture up into the world
of the living. He preferred to stay in his own
kingdom, far below. Now he turned his horses
downward, and prepared to return to his shadowy
home. But Aphrodite, the goddess of love, happened
to see him. She turned to Eros and said, "Quickly,
my son! Send one of your arrows into his lonely heart!"

4

Eros took out his straightest arrow and shot it from his bow. The arrow found its target, and Hades fell in love at once with Persephone, the maiden of spring. But Persephone's mother would never allow her daughter to become the queen of the underworld.

Persephone's mother was Demeter, the goddess of grain. Demeter was a powerful goddess. Without her blessing, grain would not grow, fruit would not ripen, crops would wither and die. But as long as she blessed the earth, the land was green and the harvest was golden.

Demeter and her daughter were seldom far from one another.
But one day, when Persephone was picking flowers in a sunny
meadow, she wandered out of her mother's sight. Suddenly,
she spotted an unusual blossom in a distant corner of the field.
But as she ran toward it, she sensed that something was wrong.

7

Just as Persephone reached the flower, the ground opened
wide. Out charged a team of horses, pulling a chariot that was
driven by Hades, god of the dead. Hades seized the frightened
maiden and swept her into the chariot. Then his horses raced
back down into the shadowy hole.

8

Persephone cried out for help. But the earth quickly closed above her, and the bright meadow was gone. The horses galloped through twisting tunnels and across dark steaming rivers—deeper and deeper into the earth. They did not stop until they had passed through the gates into the kingdom of the dead.

When Demeter heard her daughter's first cry, the goddess rushed to help her. But Persephone was gone. Demeter's eyes blazed in anger. Who would dare to steal the daughter of a goddess? Soon her anger turned to grief. And for nine days and nine nights, she searched in sorrow for her lost daughter.

Every flower seemed to remind Demeter of Persephone. Finally she went to the sun god and asked, "Who has stolen my daughter? Where is she?" The sun god replied, "Persephone sits on a throne in the kingdom of the dead. The god of the underworld has taken her for his bride."

Demeter tried to picture her lovely daughter as queen of the
lower world. It was impossible! Persephone was bright and
happy and filled with life. The kingdom of the dead was dark
and sad—a shadowy wasteland where sunlight never shined.
The thought of Persephone in the kingdom of the dead was too
much for Demeter to bear.

The goddess left her home on Mount Olympus, and went down to earth to live in loneliness. Dressed as an old woman, she wandered from place to place, silently mourning the loss of her daughter. No one recognized her. One day, she stopped to rest at a place called Eleusis.

While Demeter rested, four young maidens approached a nearby well. After they had drawn up their water from the well, they turned to the strange old woman. "Who are you?" they asked. "And why have you come to Eleusis? Perhaps we can help you."

Demeter told them that she had escaped from a band of pirates, who had taken her far from her own land. "I am a stranger here," she said. "And I know of no one who can help me."

"You must come home with us," replied the girls. "Our family has little, but we would be happy to share with you what we have." And so Demeter followed them to a nearby cottage. She went inside and was welcomed by their mother, who held a baby in her arms.

16

"Please sit down," said the mother, showing her to the best chair. But Demeter chose instead the poorest one. Then she was offered a glass of sweet wine. But she refused it, taking instead a glass of water that was flavored with mint. At length, the goddess asked if she might hold the baby. "He reminds me of my own lost child," said Demeter.

From then on, Demeter took care of the baby as if he had been her own. Each day, she fed him the food of the gods and anointed him with the perfume of the gods. Each night, she placed the child near the glowing ashes. She knew that this would make him immortal.

One night, the child's mother awoke and saw what was happening. She screamed in terror, and snatched her baby from the ashes. This made Demeter angry. "You are a fool," said the goddess. "I would have given your son immortality. He would have become a god, but now he must remain a mortal."

Suddenly, brightness and light surrounded Demeter, and she was revealed as a goddess. "I am Demeter, the goddess of grain," she said. "I am the keeper of the harvest. By your foolish act, you have displeased me. If you wish to win back my favor, you must build a great temple in my honor." Then she turned and left.

By the next morning, everyone in Eleusis had heard about the goddess and what she had said. They set to work at once, building a beautiful temple for her. When it was finished, Demeter returned and sat inside the temple. But even though the people worshiped her, she mourned more than ever for her lost daughter, Persephone.

For an entire year, Demeter did not bless the crops. She would not look with favor upon the harvest. Nothing grew, and nothing blossomed. Crops withered and died. The earth turned from green to brown. No one could find food. All over the world, people were starving.

Finally, Zeus, the king of the gods, looked down and said, "If all the mortals die, there will be no one left to worship us." He sent the other gods down, one at a time, to try to make Demeter change her mind. But it was no use. She vowed that until Persephone returned from the underworld, the earth would be barren and brown.

Then Zeus sent Hermes, the messenger god, down into the gloom of the underworld. Hermes flew through the gates into the kingdom of the dead, where he found Hades sitting on his throne. "Zeus commands that you return Persephone to the world above," said the messenger god. As soon as these words were spoken, Persephone's eyes brightened, and she sprang to her feet.

Hades knew he could not go against the wishes of Zeus, but he had an idea. He made Persephone eat a seed from a pomegranate—the food of the dead. Then he brought out his chariot and horses, and said goodbye to his queen. As soon as Persephone was safely inside the chariot, Hermes drove straight up toward the world above.

In her temple at Eleusis, Demeter still grieved for her daughter. But when she saw the chariot bearing Persephone, her sorrow quickly turned to joy. Mother and daughter embraced for the first time in more than a year. Then the goddess said, "Tell me all that has taken place. I must know everything."

And so Persephone told her mother how she had been kidnapped from the sunny meadow, carried down to the dark underworld, and made to serve as queen of the dead. When she told Demeter about the pomegranate seed, Persephone saw her mother's face grow pale. Demeter knew that anyone who tasted this food while in the lower world was doomed to return there.

But Zeus took pity on mother and daughter. Persephone had not eaten the seed willingly, so she would not have to stay in the lower world for the entire year.

For part of the year, she was allowed to stay with her mother. During those months, Demeter made the earth green and blessed the harvest. It was a time of celebration and joy.

Persephone spent the rest of each year in the lower world. During those months, Demeter mourned for her lost daughter, and she made the earth turn brown and cold. Nothing was allowed to grow. It was winter—a time for waiting. Then, each year, when Persephone returned to the world of the living, the earth turned warm and green once again.

People continued to worship Demeter at the temple in Eleusis. Soon they had regained her favor, and the goddess smiled upon them again. She taught them how to sow seeds and reap plentiful harvests, so they would have enough food to last through the barren winter months.

Then she brought forth a golden chariot and filled it with grain. She chose Triptolemus, who lived in Eleusis, as her helper, and she gave him an important task. He was to travel around the world, teaching the secrets of agriculture to mortals everywhere.

Ever since then, people have planted seeds in the spring and reaped the harvest in the fall. And to this very day, the world turns brown and barren when Persephone leaves Demeter each year. Then, when the maiden of spring returns to her mother's side, the world becomes green once again.